PRAISE

Other Taizé books published by Mowbray:

The Story of Taizé
J. L. G. Balado. (1981 Revised edition) An illustrated history.

Praise in All Our Days: Common Prayer at Taizé
Forms of Morning and Evening Prayer for every day of the year, in modern English.(1981 Revised ed.)

Psalms from Taizé
Companion volume to 'Praise in All Our Days' containing over 120 psalms in modern English.

Praying Together in Word and Song
Selection of simple meditative prayers.

Parable of Community
Basic texts including the Rule of Taizé

Brother Roger, Prior of Taizé's Personal Journal:
Festival Without End Vol.1: 1969–1970
Struggle and Contemplation Vol.2: 1970–1972
A Life We Never Dared Hope For Vol.3: 1972–1974
A Wonder of a Love Vol.4: 1974–1976

Other Books by Brother Roger, Prior of Taizé:
Living Today for God
The Dynamic of the Provisional
Violent for Peace

Books by Max Thurian, Brother of Taizé:
The Mystery of the Eucharist
Our Faith — Basic Christian Belief
Priesthood and Ministry

PRAISE
Prayers from Taizé

Extracts from "Praise in all our Days"
for personal or corporate prayer

MOWBRAY
LONDON & OXFORD

© les Presses de Taizé, 71460 Taizé Community,
   France, 1976

Translated by Emily Chisholm

First published in English in 1977
by The Faith Press; second impression
published 1980 by A. R. Mowbray & Co. Ltd.
This revised edition published 1983 by
A. R. Mowbray & Co. Ltd,
Saint Thomas House, Becket Street,
Oxford, OX1 1SJ.

ISBN 0 264 66969 X

Printed in Great Britain
by Stott Brothers Ltd., Halifax.

CONTENTS

FOREWORD

The Community of Taizé (France), over the past thirty years, has evolved a form of common prayer which is deeply biblical and firmly rooted in the liturgical traditions of the Church universal.

A completely new translation of the forms used at Taizé was edited and first published in Great Britain in 1975, and now in revised format is published by Mowbray, under the title *Praise in all our Days.*

Many people feel the need for a minimum of set forms, even in spontaneous or personal prayer. In *Praise in all our Days* they are offered an outline structure for morning and evening prayer every day. This may not be necessary for all; the present volume offers a selection of liturgical elements from *Praise in all our Days,* without an overall order of worship.

Introductions, Meditations, Intercessions, Prayers and Short Readings are grouped, covering six days and the six main liturgical celebrations—Advent, Nativity, Repentance, the Cross, Resurrection, the Holy Spirit.

Introductions and Meditations are mainly drawn from the Psalms; the Intercessions are either in the form of intercessory litanies, or in dialogue form, sometimes concerning the needs of the world, sometimes more a contemplation of Christ. Short Readings are added, so that this volume can easily be used for personal prayer; a small number of biblical Songs is also included.

A fuller introduction will be found in *Praise in all our Days,* and its comparison volume *Psalms from Taizé. Music from Taizé* containing Canons by Jacques Berthier for Assembly, choir and instruments is also available now in Great Britain.

INTRODUCTIONS

Day 1

Lord, open my lips,
— And my mouth shall proclaim your praise.
O God, come and help me,
— Lord, support and save me.

My soul pines and sighs
— For the courts of the Lord;
My heart and my flesh shout for joy
— To You, O Living God!

The sparrow has found a home
— And the swallow a nest for her young:
Your altars, Lord of all the worlds,
— My King and my God!

Happy are they who live in your house,
— They praise you for ever and ever;
Happy men whose strength is in you,
— Hearts strong for the climb to your city.

Passing through the Valley of the Weeper.
— They make it a place of wells;
They will go from height to height,
— God will appear to them in Zion.

Day 2

Lord, open my lips,
— And my mouth shall proclaim your praise.
O God, come and help me,
— Lord, support and save me.

God be gracious to us and bless us
— And smile down upon us;
The world will acknowledge your ways,
— All nations your power to save.

Let the peoples rejoice and sing,
— For you judge the world justly;
You judge the nations with equity,
— You govern the nations on the earth.

The earth has yielded her harvest,
— God, our God has blessed us.
Lord, bless us! May you be worshipped
— To all the ends of the earth.

DAY 3

Lord, open my lips,
— And my mouth shall proclaim your praise.
O God, come and help me,
— Lord, support and save me.

I lift my eyes to the hills:
where shall I find help?
— Help comes from the Lord,
— maker of heaven and earth.

He will not leave you to stumble,
your guardian never sleeps.
— No. The guardian of Israel
— never falls asleep.

The Lord guards you and shades you;
with him close at hand,
— The sun will not strike you by day.
    nor the moon at night-time.

The Lord will guard you from harm,
he will guard your soul.
— He guards your goings and comings,
    now and evermore.

DAY 4

Lord, open my lips,
— And my mouth shall proclaim your praise.
O God, come and help me,
— Lord, support and save me.

God, you are my God, I seek you at sunrise;
— My soul is thirsting for you,
My body is pining for you,
— A parched land, weary and waterless;
I long to gaze on you in the sanctuary,
— To see your glory and power.

Better than life, your love,
— My lips will speak your praise;
All my life I would bless you,
— Lift up my hands at your name;
My soul feasting till satisfied,
— Joy on my lips, praise in my mouth.

DAY 5

Lord, open my lips,
— And my mouth shall proclaim your praise.
O God, come and help me,
— Lord, support and save me.

Bring an offering and enter his House,
Worship God in the courts of his holiness,
— Fall before him, all the earth.

Go, tell the nations: God is king!
He made the worlds immovable.
— He will judge the nations justly.

Heavens, rejoice! And earth be glad!
— Let the sea roar, and all its creatures;
Let the earth rejoice and all its fruits,
— Let the forests shout for joy,

Before the Lord, for he is coming,
— He is coming to judge the earth;
He will judge the world with justice
— And the peoples with his truth.

DAY 6

Blessed be our God at all times,
now and always and for ever and ever:
— Amen.

Come, let us fall down and worship God our King:
— Come, let us fall down and worship Christ, our King and
our God.

Come, let us fall down and worship Christ among us, our King
and our God.

— God, holy; God, strong and holy; God, holy and immortal:
have pity on us.

ADVENT

Almighty Lord, come and revive us,
— Shine upon us and we shall be saved.

_____

I am listening; what does God say?
— The word from God is peace,

Peace for his People and his friends,
— All who return in sincerity.
His salvation is near those who worship him,
— His Glory will live in our land.

———

Praise to him who is coming: The King, in the name of the Lord!
— Peace in heaven and glory in the highest! Amen.

NATIVITY

Blessed be the Lord who alone has worked wonders:
— Blessed be his glorious Name for ever!

———

Such love in the heart of our God!
— The rising Sun has come to us,
Shining on those in the dark,
— Who lie in the shadow of death;

Guiding our steps into peace,
— A lamp shining in the darkness,
Until day begins to dawn
— And the morning-star rises in our hearts.

———

For us a child is born, to us the Son is given, Alleluia!
— All the ends of the earth have seen the salvation of our
    God, Alleluia!

REPENTANCE

Return to the Lord, your God,
— For he is tenderness and compassion.

———

O God of tenderness and compassion,
— O Master, slow to anger,
Full of love and full of truth,
— Turn towards me, have compassion.

13

Give your strength to your servant,
— And salvation to the child of your People;
Give me a sign of your kindness
— For Lord, you help and comfort me.

Worthy is the Lamb that was slain
to receive power and riches and wisdom,
— Strength, honour, glory and praise, Amen.

THE CROSS

Lord, do not stay away, my agony is near,
— O my strength, come quickly, help me!

Ours were the sufferings he bore,
— And ours the torments he endured.
While we thought he was punished,
— Struck down by God and disgraced.

He was pierced for our sins,
— Bruised for no fault but ours.
His punishment has won our peace,
— And by his wounds we are whole.

Lord my God, look down and answer me,
— Give light to my eyes, or they will close in death.

RESURRECTION

Give thanks to the Lord for he is good,
— For his love endures for ever, alleluia!

Open now the gates of justice:
— I will go in, I will give thanks.
This is the gate of the Lord,
— The just shall enter in.
I will give thanks, for you have heard me,
— You have saved me!

Great and marvellous are your works, Master of all!
— Right and true are your ways, King of the nations.
Who would not give praise and glory to your Name?
— For you are holy, you alone!
All the nations will come and fall before you,
— For you have done wonders upon wonders.

———

Glory, worship, wisdom, thanksgiving! Alleluia!
— Adoration, power and strength to our God! Alleluia!

THE HOLY SPIRIT

Send forth your Spirit, Lord,
— Renew the face of the earth.
Creator Spirit, come,
— Inflame our waiting hearts.
Your Spirit fills the world,
— And knows our every word.

Glory to God our Father,
— To Jesus Christ, the Son,
To you, O Holy Spirit,
— Now and for evermore.
You are, you were, you come,
— Eternal, living God!

MEDITATIONS

DAY 1

To you, Lord, I pray, you hear me every morning;
+ In the morning I rise for you, I long to see you come.
— To you, Lord . . .

O Lord, hear my words,
consider my pleading.
Hear my cry for help,
my King and my God:
— In the morning I rise for you, I long to see you come.

By the grace of your great love
I enter your house;
Low before your sanctuary
I bow, and adore:
— In the morning . . .

Great joy for all you shelter,
songs of praise for ever;
you shield and protect from harm
all who love your name:
— In the morning . . .

Lord, you bless the good,
your love defends them from evil:
— In the morning . . .

Glory to the Father, and the Son and the Holy Spirit,
— To you, Lord, I pray . . .

DAY 2

I call from my heart, answer me, my God.
— I call . . .

I will keep your commandments.
— Answer me, my God.

Glory to the Father, and the Son and the Holy Spirit.
— I call from my heart, answer me, my God.

Day 3

In my mouth he has put a new song:
+ Praise to our God!
— In my mouth . . .

I hoped in the Lord with a great hope,
he stooped down, and he heard me cry:
— Praise to our God!

Many shall see and shall fear him,
they shall believe in the Lord:
— Praise to our God!

My God, I have loved your law
from the depths of my heart:
— Praise to our God!

I have proclaimed the justice of the Lord
in the great assembly:
— Praise to our God!

Glory to the Father, and the Son and the Holy Spirit.
— In my mouth . . .

Day 4

Heal my soul, for I have sinned against you.
— Heal my soul . . .

I said: Have pity on me, Lord.
— For I have sinned against you.

Glory to the Father, and the Son and the Holy Spirit.
— Heal my soul, for I have sinned against you.

DAY 5

The Lord is with us, he is our stronghold!
+ God will help at the dawn of day.
— The Lord . . .

For us God is both refuge and strength,
there to help in time of need.
— God will help at the dawn of day.

We shall not fear, though the earth gives way,
and mountains tumble to the depths of the sea.
— God will help . . .

Come, consider the deeds of the Lord:
astounding, what he has done!
— God will help . . .

Be still and know that I am God,
exalted above the nations, exalted above the earth.
— God will help . . .

Glory to the Father, and the Son and the Holy Spirit.
— The Lord is with us . . .

DAY 6

I will bless the Lord always and everywhere.
— I will bless . . .

His praises for ever on my lips.
— Always and everywhere!

Glory to the Father, and the Son and the Holy Spirit.
— I will bless . . .

ADVENT

My soul is waiting for the Lord,
+ I am sure of his Word.
— My soul is waiting . . .

From the depths I cry to you, Lord:
hear my prayer!
— I am sure of his Word!

Forgiveness is found with you:
I hope for you in awe.
— I am sure of his Word!

My soul longs for the Lord
more than a watchman for the dawn.
— I am sure of his Word!

Let the watchman count on the dawn,
and Israel on the Lord!
— I am sure of his Word!

Glory to the Father, and the Son and the Holy Spirit.
— My soul is waiting . . .

NATIVITY

The Word was made flesh, Alleluia, Alleluia!
— The Word . . .

He dwelt among us.
— Alleluia, Alleluia!

Glory to the Father, and the Son and the Holy Spirit.
— The Word was made flesh, Alleluia, Alleluia!

REPENTANCE

Return, O Lord. Deliver my soul.
+ Save me, for the sake of your love.
— Return, O Lord . . .

Have pity on me, my strength is gone,
heal me, my bones are broken.
— Save me, for the sake of your love.

My soul is in deep distress;
Lord, how long till you return?
— Save me . . .

The Lord hears my petition,
the Lord will receive my prayer.
— Save me . . .

My enemies, routed and confounded,
will suddenly retreat in confusion.
— Save me . . .

Glory to the Father, and the Son and the Holy Spirit.
— Return, O Lord . . .

THE CROSS

All you passing by along the road, look and see if any grief can
be compared with mine.
— All you passing by . . .

My God, My God, why have you abandoned me?
— All you passing by . . .

Father, into your hands I give my spirit.
— All you passing by . . .

RESURRECTION

I am risen again, alleluia!
+ Once again I am close beside you, alleluia!
— I am risen . . .

The right hand of the Lord has done wonders,
his right hand has raised me up;
— Once again I am close beside you, alleluia!

No, I shall not die, I shall live.
I shall proclaim what God has done.
— Once again . . .

The stone which builders had rejected
has now become the corner-stone.
— Once again . . .

This is the work of God,
and wonderful in our eyes.
— Once again . . .

Glory to the Father, and the Son and the Holy Spirit.
— I am risen again . . .

THE HOLY SPIRIT

Come Holy Spirit,
From heaven shine forth with your glorious light!
— Come . . .

Come, Father of the poor; come generous Spirit;
Come, light of our hearts!
— From heaven shine forth with your glorious light!

Perfect Comforter! Wonderful Refreshment!
You make peace to dwell in our soul.
In our labour, you offer rest;
in temptation, strength;
and in our sadness, consolation.
— From heaven . . .

Most kindly, warming Light! Enter the inmost depth of our
hearts, for we are faithful to you.
Without your presence, we have nothing worthy, nothing
pure.
— From heaven . . .

Wash away our sin, send rain upon our dry ground,
heal our wounded souls.
Your fire thaw our rigidity,
kindle our apathy
and direct our wandering feet.
— From heaven . . .

On all who put their trust in you, and receive you in faith,
shower all your gifts.
Grant that they may grow in you, and persevere to the end;
give them lasting joy! Alleluia!
— Come, Holy Spirit, From heaven . . .

INTERCESSIONS

Day 1

Let us implore the mercy of the Lord:
— Deliver us, O Lord.

God of tenderness and compassion
— Deliver us, O Lord.

From injustice, from hatred and every spirit of malice:
— Deliver us, O Lord.

From war and famine, from disease and disaster:
— Deliver us, O Lord.

By the mystery of your incarnation, by your coming into the world:
— Deliver us, O Lord.

By your birth in poverty, by your baptism and your fasting in the desert:
— Deliver us, O Lord.

By Your Cross and your Passion, by your death and your burial:
— Deliver us, O Lord.

By your resurrection from the dead, by your ascension into glory:
— Deliver us, O Lord.

By the coming of the Holy Spirit the Comforter, and on the Day of judgement:
— Deliver us, O Lord.

We are sinners, give us pardon and true repentance of heart:
— Deliver us, O Lord.

DAY 2

Let us pray for the peace of the world: The Lord grant that we may live together in justice and faith.
— Lord, hear our prayer.

Let us pray for the holy Church throughout the world: The Lord keep her unshaken, founded upon the rock of his Word until the end of time.
— Lord, hear our prayer.

Let us pray for children and young people: The Lord strengthen them in their vocation.
— Lord, hear our prayer.

Let us pray for the sick: The Lord deliver them and restore the strength they need.
— Lord, hear our prayer.

Let us pray for all who are condemned to exile, prison, harsh treatment, or hard labour for the name of Christ: The Lord support them and keep them true in faith.
— Lord, hear our prayer.

Remembering all the witnesses and martyrs of the faith, all who have given their lives for God, and in communion with our brothers and sisters who have fallen asleep in Christ: Let us commit ourselves and one another to the living God through Christ our Lord.
— Lord, hear our prayer.

DAY 3

Let us pray for the whole Church, for the faithful and all who serve, that the Lord give us the grace of lives wholly consecrated to his will:
— O Lord, answer our prayer.

Let us pray for all who hate us or persecute us for Christ's sake; may the Lord calm their hatred, filling their hearts and ours with his generous love:
— O Lord, answer our prayer.

Let us pray for all who are lonely, overworked or depressed, for all who are destitute and have no-one to turn to; may the Lord protect and save in his love all who can only hope in him:
— O Lord, answer our prayer.

Let us pray for one another, and for all who are absent from us now; the Lord keep us in his grace to the end, preserve us from falling, and gather us together in his Kingdom:
— O Lord, answer our prayer.

Remembering all the witnesses and martyrs of the faith, and all who have given their lives for God, and in communion with all our brothers and sisters who have fallen asleep in Christ, let us commit ourselves and one another to the living God through his Christ:
— O Lord, answer our prayer.

Day 4

In faith let us pray to God our Father, his Son Jesus Christ and the Holy Spirit:
— O Lord, hear and have mercy (*or:* Kyrie eleison).

For the Church of the living God throughout the world let us ask for the riches of his grace;
— O Lord, hear and have mercy.

That our hearts and bodies be set free from all injustice, let us seek mercy of God:
— O Lord, hear and have mercy.

Grant peace to all who are dying, and to those who now sleep in Christ, O gracious Lord of Life:
— O Lord, hear and have mercy.

Grant us, Lord, to be fervent in believing and faithful in hope:
— O Lord, hear and have mercy.

Grant us, Lord, sincere obedience to your Word and truth in our love:
— O Lord, hear and have mercy.

Grant us, Lord, a life of thankfulness and peace:
— O Lord, hear and have mercy.

Grant us, Lord, the angel of peace and consolation, with the joy of all your saints:
— O Lord, hear and have mercy.

Day 5

Let us pray for the visible unity of Christians:
— Save us Lord; gather us from every nation.

Keep all who have found you, rooted in your love:
— May they grow in goodness and truth.

O Lord, remove our sins far from us:
— Deliver us for your name's sake.

God our defender, help us all:
— Look upon the face of your Christ.

Come soon, O Lord; how long?
— Have pity on your People's longing.

Show your work among your servants:
— May your glory shine for all mankind.

The gentleness of God be with us:
— Lord, continue what you have begun.

Day 6

Have pity, Lord, we have sinned against you:
— Pardon, Lord, for all your People.

I confess my fault before you,
and I will hide my guilt no longer:
— Search and test me, Lord,
    try my heart and my desire.

In loving kindness answer,
in your tenderness regard me:
— Forget the wrongs of my youth,
    and remember me in your love.

Bring my soul out of prison,
that I may bless your name,
— Teach me to do your will,
    lead me by your Holy Spirit.

See, God comes to my aid,
together with all who support me:
— Master, you are pardon and goodness,
    full of love for all who call you.

Remember your kindness, O Lord,
and your love—they are for ever:
— You stretch out your hand and save me,
    your right hand does all that I need.

O Wisdom, from the mouth of the Most High; you reign over all things to the ends of the earth and dispose them by the power of your love; come and teach us the way of wisdom.
— Lord Jesus, come soon!

O Lord, and Head of the house of Israel; you appeared to Moses in the fire of the burning bush and you gave him the law on Sinai; come with outstretched arm and ransom us.
— Lord Jesus, come soon.

O Branch of Jesse, standing as a sign among the nations; before you kings will keep silence, and peoples will summon you to their aid; come, set us free and delay no more.
— Lord Jesus, come soon!

O Key of David, and Sceptre of the House of Israel; you open and none can shut, you shut and none can open; come, and free the captive from prison.
— Lord Jesus, come soon!

O Morning Star, Splendour of the Light eternal and bright Sun of Justice; come and enlighten all who live in darkness, and in the shadow of death.
— Lord Jesus, come soon!

O King of the nations; you alone can fulfil their desires; Cornerstone, you make opposing nations one; come and save us. You formed us all from the clay.
— Lord Jesus, come soon!

O Emmanuel, Hope of the nations and their Saviour; come and save us, Lord our God.
— Lord Jesus, come soon!

The Spirit and the Bride say, Come!
— Amen! Lord Jesus, come soon!

Nativity

Almighty God, you have never forsaken the world when it abandoned you; from ancient times you made the promise of your victory shine before your People:
— The joy of our hearts is in God!

The patriarchs hoped for your Christ, Abraham rejoiced to see his day, foretold by the prophets and desired by all the nations:
— The joy of our hearts is in God!

The heavenly host celebrated his birth; apostles, martyrs and the faithful throughout the ages have repeated the angels' song, and now we with your whole Church praise you; for our eyes have seen your salvation:
— The joy of our hearts is in God!

Son of God, you became poor to make many rich; you humbled yourself and took the form of a slave, lifting us up to share in your glory.
— The joy of our hearts is in God!

We were in darkness and you have given us light and strength; we were without hope and we have received from your fulness grace upon grace.
— The joy of our hearts is in God!

Dispose of us as you will; make us a People who serve you in holiness; give us honest hearts to hear your word and produce in us abundant fruit to your glory.
— The joy of our hearts is in God!

Repentance

We call upon you, Lord God; you know everything, nothing escapes from you, Master of all truth:
— Be my rock and my fortress, O Lord!

You have made all the worlds and you watch over every creature . You guide to the way of life all who are living in darkness and the shadow of death:
— Be my rock . . .

It is your will to save everyone in the world, and to bring them to fulness. We offer you our praise and thanks, glorifying you with heart and voice.
— Be my rock . . .

It was your will to call us, instructing us and opening the way for us to follow. You have given us wisdom and understanding for life eternal:
— Be my rock . . .

You have ransomed us from the slavery of sin, in spite of all our wanderings, and you have given us glory and freedom:
— Be my rock...

We were dead and you gave new birth by the Spirit. We were sinners and you gave us pure hearts.
— Be my rock . . .

THE CROSS

Let us think on Jesus the Lord: instead of the joy meant for him, he endured the cross, ignoring its disgrace:
— We worship you Lord upon the Cross.

O Jesus Christ, the King of glory, born in humility to confound the proud and to raise the humble, you became the poor workman of Nazareth to teach us true wealth.
— We worship you . . .

You went among us, doing good, proclaiming the good news to the poor and freedom to prisoners.
— We worship you . . .

You came to loose the chains of every slavery, friend of the humble, bread of hungry souls, healer of the sick.
— We worship you . . .

Jesus, pattern of patience and goodness, prophet of the Kingdom of God, Master, gentle and humble of heart, forgiving all who loved much, and calling the weary and the burdened.
— We worship you . . .

Jesus, you came into the world to serve and to lay down your life, you had nowhere to lay your head, you were betrayed for money, dragged before Pilate and nailed to the Cross.
— We worship you . . .

Jesus, Lord of all the worlds by your resurrection from the dead, alive for ever to intercede with your Father and ours.
— We worship you . . .

RESURRECTION

O Christ, radiant Light, shining in our darkness. You are the most glorious of the children of men, the only Holy One among us sinners, the Source of Life who have sanctified our mortal nature:
— Son of the Living God, save us all!

You stooped low, and humbled yourself. You became obedient unto death. You walked the sorrowful road to the cross, and you call us to follow you in every moment of our lives, to death with you and to resurrection with you:
— Son . . .

You have saved us in our poverty, and won justification for us, to make us a holy nation, a People of kings and priests to God your Father:
— Son . . .

You grant us all the fulness of your grace through the gift of the Holy Spirit. Risen Lord, save us from death. Living Lord, make us sharers of your life. Conqueror, give us your victory!
— Son . . .

Burn in us all that is not kindled by your presence, and break in us all that would rebel against you, that our hearts may be fully your own as we wait for the day of your Revelation, when we shall be like you as we see you face to face.
— Son . . .

THE HOLY SPIRIT

Holy Spirit, Creator! In the beginning, you moved over the waters, and from your breath all creatures drew their life. Without you, every living creature turns to dust:
— Holy Spirit, come!

Holy Spirit, Counsellor! By your inspiration the People of God and the prophets spoke and acted in faith. You clothed them in your power, to be bearers of your Word.
— Holy Spirit, come!

Holy Spirit, Power! You overshadowed the Virgin Mary, to make her the mother of the Son of God. You prepared a pure dwelling to receive him.
— Holy Spirit, come!

Holy Spirit, Sanctifier! By you, Jesus grew in wisdom and grace. On the day of his baptism, you descended on him as a dove to consecrate him and you armed him with power to bear witness to the Father.
— Holy Spirit, come!

PRAYERS

Day 1

Eternal Word of the Father; for our salvation you became one with us in everything but sin. Give us the light of your liberating word, may we not only hear it, but act upon it; and so lead us into God's Kingdom where you live and reign for ever, — Amen.

Day 2

O Lord, you promise that all whose hearts are clear shall see God; dispel the darkness and confusion of our hearts, and in your light we shall see eternal light, now and ever, — Amen.

Day 3

O Christ, our Lord; you are the way, the truth and the life: apart from you, we go astray, we cannot understand, and life without you is no life at all. Watch over our thoughts, our words and our actions, keep us throughout this day, so that all we do may be begun and completed in your name, blessed for ever and ever, — Amen.

Day 4

Lord our God, King of heaven and earth; sanctify today our hearts and our bodies, all that we undertake, and everyone we meet; may we live according to your will and bear the fruits of your Kingdom, through Jesus Christ, our Lord, — Amen.

Day 5

O Lord, our sole refuge and our only hope; give us grace to consecrate ourselves tirelessly to your service in a great love for you and for our brothers, until that day when we come to the blessed vision of your face and you wipe away every tear from our eyes, in the Kingdom of Christ, our Lord. — Amen.

Day 6

Lord Jesus Christ, light shining in our darkness; have mercy on our tired and doubting hearts. Renew in us the courage we need, to bring to completion the work your calling has begun in us. Freely you gave your life on the Cross, freely you took it again in your Resurrection, you live and reign now, and for ever, — Amen.

Advent

O Christ, splendour of the glory of God and perfect image of the Father; we give you thanks for the infinite love which sent you among us; we confess you light and life of the world; and we adore you as our Lord and our God, now and for ever,
— Amen.

Nativity

Lord Christ, your light shines in our darkness, giving gladness in our sorrow and a presence in our isolation; we pray you to fill our lives with your mystery, until our hearts overflow with gladness and praise, for you are the beginning and end of all that exists, and you live for evermore. — Amen.

REPENTANCE

God our Father, you so loved the world that you sent your only Son to be our Salvation. Kindle in our hearts that same love with which Christ loves us, now and for ever, — Amen.

THE CROSS

Lord, we pray you, look upon your family for whom our Lord Jesus Christ was willing to undergo the torture of the Cross. Now he reigns with you and the Holy Spirit for ever,
— Amen.

RESURRECTION

Lord Jesus Christ, you are the shepherd and we are your flock; protect us all, and save us from every danger; fulfil your promise and be with us at every moment, that we may come to bless your Name in the light of our resurrection, in your Kingdom which will have no end, — Amen.

THE HOLY SPIRIT

Father, of your infinite goodness, set us aflame with that fire of the Spirit Christ brought upon the earth and longed to see ablaze, for he lives and reigns with you and the Spirit now and for ever, — Amen.

SHORT READINGS

DAY 1

Jesus said, "Do not judge, and you will not be judged; do not condemn, and you will not be condemned; forgive, and you will be forgiven. Give, and you will receive; good measure, pressed down, shaken together, brimming over, will be poured out for you; the measure you give is the measure you will receive." (Luke 6.)

DAY 2

Jesus took Peter, James and John, and led them up a high mountain, by themselves. And he was transfigured before them, his face shone like the sun and his clothes became dazzling as light. They saw Moses and Elijah appear and talk with him . . . A bright cloud overshadowed them and a voice from the cloud proclaimed, "This is my Son, my Beloved, on whom all my favour rests; listen to him". (Matthew 17.)

DAY 3

Someone said to Jesus, "I will follow you, wherever you go". Jesus answered, "Foxes have their holes, and the birds have nests; but the Son of Man has nowhere to lay his head".
To another, Jesus said, "Follow me!" but he answered, "First, let me go and bury my father". Jesus said, "Let the dead bury the dead; you, go and announce the Kingdom of God".
Someone else said, "Lord, I will follow you; but first let me take leave of my people". Jesus replied, "No one who sets his hand to the plough and then looks back is fit for the Kingdom of God". (Luke 9.)

Day 4

Jesus said, "Whoever eats my flesh and drinks my blood has eternal life and I will raise him up on the last day. My flesh is truly food; my blood is truly drink. Whoever eats my flesh and drinks my blood dwells in me and I in him." (John 6.)

Day 5

Jesus said, "There is no one who has given up home, brothers or sisters, father or mother, children or land, for my sake and the Gospel's, who will not receive in this age a hundred times as much—houses, brothers and sisters, mothers and children and land—with persecutions; and in the age to come eternal life." (Mark 10.)

Day 6

A dispute arose among the disciples: which of them was the greatest? Jesus knew what was passing in their minds, so he took a child by the hand and stood him at his side, and said, "Whoever receives this child in my name receives me; and whoever receives me receives him who sent me. For the least among you, he is the greatest." (Luke 9.)

Advent

Arise, Jerusalem, rise clothed in light; your light has come and the glory of the Lord shines over you. Though darkness covers the earth and dark night the nations, the Lord shall shine upon you and over you shall his glory appear; and the nations shall march towards your light. (Isaiah 60.)

NATIVITY

Have that bearing towards one another which was also in Christ Jesus: by nature divine, he did not retain for himself his rank as equal with God, but poured out his glory in love, becoming a humble slave and living the life of a man. (Philippians 2.)

REPENTANCE

Jesus said, "The Kingdom of Heaven is like treasure lying buried in a field; a man finds it, buries it once more and, full of joy, goes to sell everything he has and buys that field. Or, the Kingdom of Heaven is like a merchant in search of fine pearls; he finds one of great value, so he goes and sells everything he has, and buys it." (Matthew 13.)

THE CROSS

Jesus said, "Father, forgive them, they do not know what they are doing." "I thirst." "My God, my God, why have you forsaken me?" "Father, into your hands I give my spirit." "It is done." (John 19 . . .)

RESURRECTION

He is the Image of the unseen God, the Firstborn of all creation. For in him all things were made, in heaven and on the earth. All was created through him and for him, he was before all things, and everything exists in him. He is also the Head of his Body, the Church, he is the Beginning, the Firstborn from the dead. God meant all his fullness to live in him, and reconciled through him all creation to himself: everything on earth and everything in the heavens, all gathered into peace by his death on the Cross. (Colossians 1.)

THE HOLY SPIRIT

All who are moved by the Spirit of God are sons of God; the Spirit you have received is not a spirit of slavery, leading you back into a life of fear, but a Spirit that makes us sons, able to cry "Abba! Father!". (Romans 8.)

PSALMS AND SONGS

PSALM

Come, sing to the Lord a new song,
sing to the Lord, all the earth,
sing for him, and bless his name.

Proclaim his salvation day by day,
and tell his glory to the world,
to all peoples his marvellous deeds.

God is great and worthy of all praise,
to be feared above all gods,
the gods of the nations are nought.

It is God who made the heavens,
where glory and majesty attend,
around him beauty and strength.

So praise the Lord, every land,
sing praises for his glory and power,
give praise to the glory of his name.

PSALM

Come, shout for joy to the Lord,
and sing to the Rock who saves;
with thanksgiving, come before him,
give praise with music and song.

Great is the Lord, he is God,
a great king above all gods;
in his hands are the depths of the earth,
and the heights of the mountains are his;
his the sea, for he made it,
and the earth, shaped by his power.

Enter in, bend low, bow down,
let us kneel before God our Maker;
for he is our God and we
the people whose Shepherd he is,
the flock he leads with his hand.

Today, if you would hear his voice?
Do not harden your hearts as at the Rock,
on that day of temptation in the desert,
when your fathers tested and proved me,
although they had witnessed my deeds.

PSALM

When the Lord brought our prisoners home,
    it felt like a dream!
Every mouth was filled with laughter,
    and our lips with songs!

In other lands, people said: What wonders
    the Lord has done for them!
The Lord has done marvels indeed,
    how great is our joy!

Bring back our captives, O Lord,
    like streams after rain;
then the sowers who sowed in tears
    will harvest in joy.

They went out with sobbing and tears
    when the seed was sown;
now they come with laughter and with songs,
    for the sheaves are gathered!

SONG OF MARY

My soul sings praises to the Lord,
my spirit glorifies my Saviour, my God!

For he has stooped to his humble servant,
and henceforth all the ages will call me greatly blessed.
The Almighty chose me for his wonders;
Holy his Name!

And his love endures through the ages
to all who revere him;
he displays the strength of his arm,
and he scatters the conceited.

He topples all the powerful from their throne,
and he raises the humble.
He feasts all the hungry with good things,
but the rich go empty-handed.

He lifts up his own servant Israel,
ever remembering his love,
his ancient promise made to our fathers
in his oath to Abraham and to his race evermore.

Praise to Father, Son and Holy Spirit,
now and in the time to come
and for ever and ever.

SONG OF ZECHARIAH

Blessed be the Lord God of Israel,
coming to ransom his People;

Raising up saving power
in the house of his servant David,
as he said by the mouth of his prophets,
his saints in days of old:

He sets us free from oppression,
free from the hands of our foes;
his bond of love with our fathers,
his covenant binding for ever;

His oath to our father Abraham,
assuring us, that liberated from fear,
delivered from all oppression,
we serve him in goodness and love,
before him, throughout our days.

And you, to be called his prophet,
will walk in the presence of God,
to prepare the ways he shall come,
announcing his People's salvation
with pardon for all their sins.

Through the love in the heart of our God,
the Rising Sun will come to us,
shining on those in the dark
who lie in the shadow of death,
and guiding our steps into peace.

THE BEATITUDES

Happy the poor in heart, the Kingdom of Heaven is theirs.
Happy the gentle, they will share in the Promised Land.
Happy all who weep, they will be comforted.
Happy are the hungry and thirsty for justice, they will be
filled.
Happy the merciful, mercy will be theirs.

Happy the clear in heart, they will see God.

Happy the creators of peace, they will be called Sons of God.

Happy all who are persecuted for what is right, the Kingdom of Heaven is theirs.

Happy are you, if they persecute you, if they slander you because of Christ: be glad and leap for joy, for your reward in heaven is great!